STEP-BY-STEP

SAUCES

GREENWICH EDITIONS

Specially produced for Greenwich Editions
Unit 7, 202-208 New North Road
London, N1 7BJ

© Salamander Books Ltd., 1995

ISBN 0 862 880 36X

Author: Anne Sheasby
Photographer: Simon Butcher

Printed and bound in Slovenia

OTHER TITLES IN THIS SERIES:

Step-by-Step Chinese Cookery
Step-by-Step Fondues
Step-by-Step Indian Cookery
Step-by-Step Pasta Dishes
Step-by-Step Pizzas
Step-by-Step Tapas & Spanish Cookery
Step-by-Step Thai Cookery
Step-by-Step Vegetarian Cookery
Step-by-Step Wok Cookery

CONTENTS

INTRODUCTION

A good sauce will provide the finishing touch to numerous dishes. A sauce enhances the flavour of food, both sweet and savoury, and can transform a dish into something special.

Many sauces are traditionally associated with certain foods, but sauces are also very versatile and can be served with a wide variety of dishes. More unusual sauces can make a pleasant change and by choosing different ingredients, you can create appetising sauces to suit all kinds of foods and tastes.

Sauces are simple to make once the basic techniques have been mastered and they don't need to be high in calories or fat to make them appealing and delicious. By replacing some of the more traditional ingredients with lower calorie/lower fat alternatives, you can create light, healthy sauces, full of delicious flavours, colours and textures. You will be reducing your calorie and fat intakes, without even noticing the difference.

In this book, you will discover tasty light sauces, both sweet and savoury. Recipes include traditional sauces as well as more unusual light sauces and each recipe is illustrated in full colour with step-by-step instructions, showing you just what to expect.

Try some of these delicious light sauces and add that special finishing touch to your own dishes.

INGREDIENTS FOR LIGHT SAUCES

Nowadays, healthy eating is a very important part of our everyday lives and following basic, good, healthy eating patterns is essential for our general well-being.

Sauces are often thought of as the delicious, creamy, rich accompaniment to numerous dishes. Traditionally, many sauces are relatively high in calories and fat, but light sauces just as delicious and appetising can be made by making a few simple changes to the ingredients in the recipe, resulting in lower calorie/lower fat light sauces.

By reducing the amount of fat, sugar and salt you eat and increasing the amount of fibre in your diet, you will be making small changes in your eating habits, whilst taking positive steps towards eating a healthier diet.

The recipes use a whole range of different ingredients, all of which are widely and readily available.

LOW FAT

Low fat spread, skimmed or semi-skimmed milk, reduced fat creams and lower fat cheeses, have been used in place of some of the higher calorie and higher fat traditional ingredients, often used in sauce-making.

Low fat plain yogurt is a tasty, healthy alternative to milk or cream in some of the light sauces.

In place of butter or margarine, which contain very high fat contents, some of the recipes use low fat spread as an alternative. Low fat spread contains half the fat of butter or margarine and is suitable for melting. Low fat spreads do vary and you may need to experiment to see which one you like best. Very low fat spread is not suitable for sauces.

Oil has been used in some of the recipes, but only the polyunsaturated varieties such as sunflower oil, sesame oil and olive oil. Oils are high in

calories and fat and should be used sparingly. It is possible to reduce the amount of oil that would traditionally be used in many sauces and dressings without affecting the flavour or texture of the light sauce, as well as keeping it lower in calories and fat.

FRUIT AND VEGETABLES

Fruit and vegetable purées make an excellent low calorie/low fat basis for many light sauces and they add delightful flavours, colours and textures to many dishes, as well as increasing the dietary fibre content of the meal.

Fresh fruits have been used in the recipes as much as possible, as they are full of natural sugar and flavour.

When canned fruit has been used in recipes, use canned fruit in fruit juice rather than in syrup.

Fresh herbs and spices add delicious flavours and aromas to many of the light sauces, without adding many calories or fat.

SERVING SUGGESTIONS

Serving suggestions appear at the end of each recipe, but use your imagination – many of the light sauces are very versatile and can be served with a wide variety of dishes. Many of the recipes are suitable for vegetarians too.

Each recipe shows the total amount of light sauce the recipe makes, as well as calorie and fat contents of each recipe per tablespoon of the cooked light sauce.

BASIC WHITE SAUCE

25 g (1 oz/6 teaspoons) low fat spread
25 g (1 oz/¼ cup) plain flour
300 ml (10 fl oz/1¼ cups) semi-skimmed milk
salt and pepper

In a saucepan, melt low fat spread over a low heat. Stir in flour and cook for 1 minute, stirring.

Remove pan from heat and gradually stir or whisk in the milk. Bring slowly to the boil, stirring or whisking, and continue to cook until the mixture thickens.

Simmer gently for 3 minutes. Remove pan from heat and season with salt and pepper. Serve with meat, poultry, fish or vegetables.

Makes 300 ml (10 fl oz/1¼ cups/20 tbsp).

Calories per tablespoon: 16 Kcals/67 Kj
Fat per tablespoon: 0.7 g

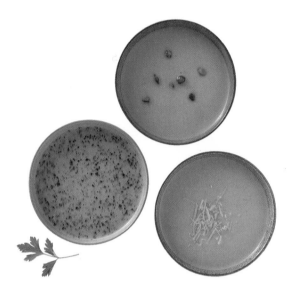

— WHITE SAUCE VARIATIONS —

CHEESE SAUCE
Follow the recipe for Basic White Sauce.
Before seasoning with salt and pepper, stir in
55 g (2 oz/½ cup) grated reduced-fat Cheddar
cheese and 1 teaspoon prepared mustard.
Serve with fish, poultry, ham, vegetables or
egg dishes.

Calories per tablespoon: 23 Kcals/98 Kj
Fat per tablespoon: 1.2 g

PARSLEY SAUCE
Follow the recipe for Basic White Sauce.
After seasoning with salt and pepper, stir in 2
tablespoons finely chopped fresh parsley.
Serve with fish, ham or bacon.

Calories per tablespoon: 16 Kcals/67 Kj
Fat per tablespoon: 0.7 g

CAPER SAUCE
Follow the recipe for Basic White Sauce.
Before seasoning with salt and pepper, stir in
2 tablespoons capers and 2 teaspoons vinegar
from the jar of capers. Reheat gently before
serving. Serve with lamb.

Calories per tablespoon: 16 Kcals/67 Kj
Fat per tablespoon: 0.7 g

ESPAGNOLE SAUCE

1 rasher lean back bacon
25 g (1 oz/6 teaspoons) low fat spread
1 small onion or shallot
1 small carrot
55 g (2 oz) mushrooms
9 teaspoons plain flour
550 ml (20 fl oz/2½ cups) beef stock
1 bouquet garni
4 black peppercorns
1 bay leaf
2 tablespoons tomato purée (paste)
salt and pepper

Trim the rind and fat from the bacon and chop the bacon finely.

In a saucepan, melt low fat spread over a low heat. Add bacon and cook for 2 minutes, stirring. Chop onion or shallot, carrot and mushrooms finely. Add vegetables to the bacon and cook for 5-10 minutes until lightly browned, stirring occasionally. Stir in flour and cook until lightly browned, stirring continuously. Remove pan from heat and gradually stir in stock. Add all the remaining ingredients and bring slowly to the boil, stirring, until the mixture thickens. Cover and simmer gently for 1 hour, stirring occasionally.

Strain the sauce, remove bouquet garni and rub the pulp through a sieve. Discard the remaining pulp and return sauce to a saucepan. Reheat gently and adjust the seasoning before serving. Serve with red meats or game.

Makes 425 ml (15 fl oz/1¾ cups/28 tbsp).

Calories per tablespoon: 12 Kcals/50 Kj
Fat per tablespoon: 0.5 g

BÉCHAMEL SAUCE

1 small onion or shallot
1 small carrot
½ stick celery
1 bay leaf
6 black peppercorns
several stalks parsley
300 ml (10 fl oz/1¼ cups) semi-skimmed milk
25 g (1 oz/6 teaspoons) low fat spread
25 g (1 oz/¼ cup) plain flour
salt and pepper

Slice the onion or shallot and carrot. Chop the celery roughly. Put vegetables and flavourings in a saucepan with milk and bring slowly to the boil.

Remove pan from heat, cover and set aside to infuse for 30 minutes. Strain into a jug, reserving the milk. In a saucepan, melt low fat spread over a low heat. Stir in flour and cook for 1 minute, stirring.

Remove pan from heat and gradually stir or whisk in flavoured milk. Bring slowly to the boil, stirring or whisking, and continue to cook until the mixture thickens. Simmer gently for 3 minutes. Remove pan from heat and season with salt and pepper. Serve with poultry, fish, vegetables or egg dishes.

Makes 300 ml (10 fl oz/1¼ cups/20 tbsp).

Calories per tablespoon: 18 Kcals/75 Kj
Fat per tablespoon: 0.8 g

──── TRADITIONAL GRAVY ────

1 small onion
25 g (1 oz/6 teaspoons) low fat spread
25 g (1 oz/¼ cup) plain flour
300 ml (10 fl oz/1¼ cups) beef stock
1 tablespoon tomato purée (paste)
1 teaspoon sugar
1 teaspoon yeast extract
1 teaspoon dried mixed herbs
salt and pepper

Chop onion finely. In a saucepan, melt low fat spread over a low heat. Add onion and cook for 5 minutes until soft, stirring.

Stir in flour and cook gently for 1 minute, stirring. Remove pan from heat and gradually stir in stock. Add the remaining ingredients and bring slowly to the boil, stirring. Continue to cook until the mixture thickens, then simmer gently for 3 minutes.

Adjust the seasoning and serve with grilled or roast red meats, such as beef, lamb or pork.

Makes 425 ml (15 fl oz/1¾ cups/28 tbsp).

Calories per tablespoon: 9 Kcals/36 Kj
Fat per tablespoon: 0.4 g

Variation: Use chicken stock instead of beef stock, if serving the gravy with poultry.

ONION SAUCE

1 onion
25 g (1 oz/6 teaspoons) low fat spread
25 g (1 oz/¼ cup) plain flour
450 ml (16 fl oz/2 cups) semi-skimmed milk
salt and pepper

Chop onion finely. In a saucepan, melt low fat spread over a low heat. Add onion and cook for 8-10 minutes, until soft, stirring occasionally.

Stir in flour and cook for 1 minute, stirring. Remove pan from heat and gradually stir in milk. Bring slowly to the boil, stirring, and continue to cook until the mixture thickens.

Simmer gently for 3 minutes. Remove pan from heat and season with salt and pepper. Serve with lamb or egg dishes.

Makes 550 ml (20 fl oz/2½ cups/36 tbsp).

Calories per tablespoon: 12 Kcals/50 Kj
Fat per tablespoon: 0.5 g

TARRAGON SAUCE

25 g (1 oz/6 teaspoons) low fat spread
25 g (1 oz/¼ cup) plain flour
300 ml (10 fl oz/1¼ cups) chicken stock
150 ml (5 fl oz/⅔ cup) semi-skimmed milk
2 tablespoons tarragon vinegar
few sprigs tarragon
2 teaspoons smooth mustard
55 g (2 oz/½ cup) reduced-fat Cheddar cheese
salt and pepper

In a saucepan, melt low fat spread over a low heat. Stir in flour and cook for 1 minute, stirring. Remove pan from heat and gradually stir or whisk in stock, milk and vinegar.

Bring slowly to the boil, stirring or whisking, and continue to cook until the mixture thickens. Simmer gently for 3 minutes. Chop the tarragon finely.

Stir the tarragon into the sauce with the mustard, cheese and salt and pepper and reheat gently, but do not allow the mixture to boil. Serve with chicken or turkey.

Makes 550 ml (20 fl oz/2½ cups/36 tbsp).

Calories per tablespoon: 11 Kcals/47 Kj
Fat per tablespoon: 0.6 g

MUSTARD SAUCE

25 g (1 oz/6 teaspoons) low fat spread
25 g (1 oz/¼ cup) plain flour
300 ml (10 fl oz/1¼ cups) semi-skimmed milk
6 teaspoons wholegrain mustard
salt and pepper

In a saucepan, melt low fat spread over a low heat. Stir in flour and cook for 1 minute, stirring.

Remove pan from heat and gradually stir or whisk in the milk. Bring slowly to the boil, stirring or whisking, and continue to cook until mixture thickens. Simmer gently for 3 minutes.

Stir in mustard and season with salt and pepper. Reheat gently before serving. Serve with oily fish, ham, bacon, vegetables or cheese dishes.

Makes 350 ml (12 fl oz/1½ cups/23 tbsp).

Calories per tablespoon: 15 Kcals/64 Kj
Fat per tablespoon: 0.8 g

—LEMON & CHERVIL SAUCE—

25 g (1 oz/6 teaspoons) low fat spread
9 teaspoons plain flour
150 ml (5 fl oz/²⁄₃ cup) chicken stock
150 ml (5 fl oz/²⁄₃ cup) semi-skimmed milk
few sprigs chervil
finely grated rind and juice of 1 lemon
salt and pepper

In a saucepan, melt low fat spread over a low heat. Stir in flour and cook for 1 minute, stirring. Remove pan from heat and gradually stir or whisk in stock and milk.

Bring slowly to the boil, stirring or whisking, and continue to cook until the mixture thickens. Simmer gently for 3 minutes. Chop chervil finely.

Stir chervil into sauce with lemon rind and lemon juice and season with salt and pepper. Reheat the sauce gently before serving. Serve with fish such as cod, haddock, plaice or salmon.

Makes 300 ml (10 fl oz/1 ¼ cups/20 tbsp).

Calories per tablespoon: 17 Kcals/70 Kj
Fat per serving: 0.7 g

MUSHROOM SAUCE

1 small onion
1 small carrot
½ stick celery
1 bay leaf
6 black peppercorns
450 ml (16 fl oz/2 cups) semi-skimmed milk
175 g (6 oz) button mushrooms
55 g (2 oz/¼ cup) low fat spread
55 g (2 oz/½ cup) plain flour
salt and pepper

Slice the onion and carrot. Chop celery roughly. Put vegetables and flavourings in a saucepan with the milk and slowly bring to the boil.

Remove pan from heat, cover and set aside to infuse for 30 minutes. Strain into a jug, reserving the milk. Slice mushrooms thinly. In a saucepan, melt low fat spread over a low heat. Add mushrooms and cook for 5 minutes until soft, stirring occasionally. Stir in flour and cook for 1 minute, stirring. Remove pan from heat and gradually stir in the flavoured milk.

Bring slowly to the boil, stirring, and continue to cook until the mixture thickens. Simmer gently for 3 minutes. Remove pan from heat and season with salt and pepper. Serve with fish or vegetables such as broccoli or potatoes.

Makes 550 ml (20 fl oz/2½ cups/36 tbsp).

Calories per tablespoon: 18 Kcals/75 Kj
Fat per tablespoon: 0.9 g

CELERY SAUCE

1 small onion
225 g (8 oz) celery
25 g (1 oz/6 teaspoons) low fat spread
25 g (1 oz/¼ cup) plain flour
150 ml (5 fl oz/⅔ cup) semi-skimmed milk
150 ml (5 fl oz/⅔ cup) vegetable stock
salt and pepper

Chop onion and celery finely. In a saucepan, melt low fat spread over a low heat.

Add onion and celery to pan and cook for 8-10 minutes until soft, stirring occasionally. Stir in flour and cook for 1 minute, stirring. Remove pan from heat and gradually stir in milk and stock. Bring slowly to the boil, stirring, and continue to cook until the mixture thickens.

Simmer gently for 3 minutes. Remove pan from heat and season with salt and pepper. Serve with roast chicken or turkey.

Makes 550 ml (20 fl oz/2½ cups/36 tbsp).

Calories per tablespoon: 8 Kcals/34 Kj
Fat per tablespoon: 0.4 g

RED WINE SAUCE

1 small onion
1 clove garlic
25 g (1 oz/6 teaspoons) low fat spread
25 g (1 oz/¼ cup) plain flour
250 ml (9 fl oz/1 cup) beef stock
200 ml (7 fl oz/¾ cup) red wine
2 teaspoons chopped fresh thyme
1 tablespoon lemon juice
salt and pepper

Grate onion finely and crush garlic. In a saucepan, melt low fat spread over a low heat. Add onion and garlic and cook for 5 minutes, stirring occasionally.

Stir in flour and cook for 1 minute, stirring. Remove pan from heat and gradually stir in stock and wine. Bring slowly to the boil, stirring, and continue to cook until the mixture thickens. Simmer gently for 3 minutes.

Stir the chopped thyme into the sauce with the lemon juice and season with salt and pepper. Reheat the sauce gently before serving. Serve with beef.

Makes 500 ml (18 fl oz/2¼ cups/33 tbsp).

Calories per tablespoon: 10 Kcals/41 Kj
Fat per tablespoon: 0.3 g

Variation: Use medium white wine in place of the red wine for a white wine sauce and serve it with poultry or fish.

——QUICK TOMATO SAUCE——

1 clove garlic
1 tablespoon chopped mixed fresh herbs, such as
    parsley, thyme, rosemary and chives
400 g (14 oz) can chopped tomatoes
150 ml (5 fl oz/²/₃ cup) dry white wine
1 tablespoon tomato purée (paste)
salt and pepper
3 teaspoons cornflour

Crush garlic. Put garlic, herbs, tomatoes, wine, tomato purée (paste) and salt and pepper in a saucepan and mix well.

Bring slowly to the boil, cover and simmer gently for 20 minutes, stirring occasionally. In a small bowl, blend the cornflour with 1 tablespoon water.

Stir cornflour mixture into tomato sauce, mixing well and bring the sauce back to the boil, stirring. Simmer gently for 3 minutes. Adjust the seasoning before serving. Serve with fish, meat or poultry.

Makes 550 ml (20 fl oz/2½ cups/36 tbsp).

Calories per tablespoon: 6 Kcals/25 Kj
Fat per tablespoon: 0.02 g

—————— WATERCRESS SAUCE ——————

1 small onion
1 clove garlic
2 bunches watercress
25 g (1 oz/6 teaspoons) low fat spread
25 g (1 oz/¼ cup) plain flour
300 ml (10 fl oz/1¼ cups) semi-skimmed milk
150 ml (5 fl oz/⅔ cup) chicken stock
salt and pepper

Chop onion finely. Crush garlic and chop watercress finely. In a saucepan, melt low fat spread over a low heat. Add onion, garlic and watercress and cook for 5 minutes until soft, stirring occasionally.

Stir in flour and cook for 1 minute, stirring. Remove pan from heat and gradually stir or whisk in milk and stock and season with salt and pepper. Bring slowly to the boil, stirring or whisking, and continue to cook until the mixture thickens. Cover and simmer gently for 5 minutes. Remove pan from heat and set aside to cool.

When cool, purée the sauce in a blender or food processor until smooth. Return the sauce to a saucepan, reheat gently and adjust the seasoning before serving. Serve with lamb, fish or savoury pies or quiches.

Makes 550 ml (20 fl oz/2½ cups/36 tbsp).

Calories per tablespoon: 8 Kcals/34 Kj
Fat per tablespoon: 0.4 g

—SWEET RED PEPPER SAUCE—

2 red peppers (capsicums) (see Note)
6 spring onions
2 cloves garlic
1 sprig rosemary
300 ml (10 fl oz/1¼ cups) vegetable stock
salt and pepper

Seed peppers (capsicums) and chop finely.
Trim and slice spring onions thinly. Crush
garlic and chop rosemary finely. Put peppers
(capsicums), spring onions, garlic, rosemary,
stock and salt and pepper in a saucepan.

Bring mixture slowly to the boil, cover and
simmer for 20 minutes until the vegetables
are soft, stirring occasionally. Remove pan
from heat and set aside to cool. Once cool,
purée the sauce in a blender or food processor until smooth. Return the sauce to a
saucepan.

Reheat gently and adjust the seasoning before
serving. Serve hot or cold with vegetable
dishes such as a vegetable terrine.

Makes 500 ml (18 fl oz/2¼ cups/33 tbsp).

Calories per tablespoon: 4 Kcals/17 Kj
Fat per tablespoon: 0.06 g

Note: The peppers (capsicums) may be
peeled if wished. Place under a hot grill and
cook for 8-10 minutes, turning frequently.
Rub skins off under cold water.

— SAGE & RED ONION SAUCE —

2 red onions
25 g (1 oz/6 teaspoons) low fat spread
25 g (1 oz/¼ cup) plain flour
150 ml (5 fl oz/⅔ cup) semi-skimmed milk
juice of 1 lime
2 tablespoons chopped fresh sage
salt and pepper

Chop onions finely. Put onions in a saucepan with 300 ml (10 fl oz/1¼ cups) water. Bring to the boil, cover and simmer gently for 10 minutes until the onions are soft. Strain onions, reserving 150 ml (5 fl oz/⅔ cup) of the cooking liquid.

In a saucepan, melt low fat spread over a low heat. Add onions and cook for 5 minutes, stirring. Stir in flour and cook for 1 minute, stirring. Remove pan from the heat and gradually stir in reserved stock, the milk and lime juice.

Bring slowly to the boil, stirring, and continue to cook until the mixture thickens. Simmer gently for 3 minutes. Remove pan from heat. Stir chopped sage into sauce. Season with salt and pepper, mixing well. Serve with poultry or game.

Makes 500 ml (18 fl oz/2¼ cups/33 tbsp).

Calories per tablespoon: 11 Kcals/47 Kj
Fat per tablespoon: 0.4 g

CHILLI SAUCE

4 spring onions
1 red chilli
1 clove garlic
3 teaspoons peanut oil
400 g (14 oz) can chopped tomatoes
1 tablespoon lemon juice
3 teaspoons soft brown sugar
salt and pepper
2 teaspoons cornflour

Trim and chop spring onions finely. Seed and chop chilli finely and crush garlic.

In a saucepan, heat oil for 1 minute. Add onions, chilli and garlic and cook for 5 minutes, stirring. Add tomatoes, lemon juice, sugar and salt and pepper. Bring slowly to the boil, cover and simmer gently for 10 minutes, stirring occasionally.

In a small bowl, blend cornflour with 1 tablespoon water. Stir cornflour mixture into the chilli sauce and bring the sauce to the boil, stirring continuously. Simmer gently for 3 minutes and adjust the seasoning before serving. Serve with fish, seafood or stuffed vegetables.

Makes 450 ml (16 fl oz/2 cups/30 tbsp).

Calories per tablespoon: 11 Kcals/47 Kj
Fat per tablespoon: 0.5 g

— SPINACH & GARLIC SAUCE —

300 g (10 oz) fresh spinach
150 ml (5 fl oz/²⁄₃ cup) vegetable stock
4 cloves garlic
1 tablespoon chopped mixed fresh herbs, such as
    parsley, thyme, rosemary and chives
1 teaspoon ground cumin
salt and pepper

Chop spinach roughly and place in a sauce-pan with stock. Cover the saucepan, bring the mixture to the boil and boil for 5 minutes until spinach is soft. Crush garlic cloves.

Stir garlic, herbs, cumin and salt and pepper into the spinach mixture, mixing well. Bring slowly to the boil, cover and simmer gently for 10 minutes, stirring occasionally. Remove the pan from the heat and set aside to cool.

Once cool, purée the sauce in a blender or food processor until smooth. Return the sauce to a saucepan. Reheat gently and adjust the seasoning before serving. Serve with beef, fish or egg dishes.

Makes 500 ml (18 fl oz/2¼ cups/33 tbsp).

Calories per tablespoon: 3 Kcals/12 Kj
Fat per tablespoon: 0.1 g

CURRY SAUCE

1 onion
1 clove garlic
2 teaspoons sunflower oil
225 g (8 oz) potatoes
225 g (8 oz) can chopped tomatoes
300 ml (10 fl oz/1¼ cups) vegetable stock
3 teaspoons curry powder
1 teaspoon ground bay leaves
salt and pepper
55 g (2 oz/⅓ cup) sultanas

Chop onion finely and crush garlic. In a saucepan, heat oil for 1 minute. Add onion and garlic and cook for 5 minutes, stirring.

Peel and grate potatoes coarsely. Add potatoes, tomatoes, stock, curry powder, ground bay leaves and salt and pepper to the saucepan and mix well. Bring slowly to the boil, cover and simmer gently for 30 minutes, stirring occasionally. Remove pan from the heat and set aside to cool. Once cool, purée the sauce in a blender or food processor until smooth.

Return the sauce to a saucepan and add the sultanas. Reheat gently and adjust the seasoning before serving. Serve with vegetables or egg dishes.

Makes 800 ml (28 fl oz/3½ cups/53 tbsp).

Calories per tablespoon: 11 Kcals/47 Kj
Fat per tablespoon: 0.2 g

Variation: The sultanas can be added with the potatoes and tomatoes and puréed, if preferred.

HORSERADISH SAUCE

4 tablespoons grated fresh horseradish
1 teaspoon caster sugar
2 teaspoons smooth mustard
salt and pepper
2 tablespoons malt vinegar
9 teaspoons low fat plain yogurt

Place the grated horseradish in a bowl.
Add sugar, mustard and salt and pepper and
mix well.

Stir in vinegar, then gently stir in the yogurt,
mixing well. Leave the horseradish sauce in a
cool place for 30 minutes before serving, to
allow the flavours to develop.

Serve with beef or oily fish.

Makes 150 ml (5 fl oz/²/₃ cup/10 tbsp).

Calories per tablespoon: 10 Kcals/41 Kj
Fat per tablespoon: 0.1 g

Variation: Use reduced fat single (light)
cream in place of the plain yogurt, but
remember this will increase the calorie and
fat contents of the sauce.

Calories per tablespoon: 13 Kcals/53 Kj
Fat per tablespoon: 0.5 g

SPICY COURGETTE SAUCE

2 courgettes (zucchini)
1 green pepper (capsicum)
1 small onion
1 clove garlic
25 g (1 oz/6 teaspoons) low fat spread
1 teaspoon ground coriander
½ teaspoon ground cumin
½ teaspoon ground chilli powder
¼ teaspoon cayenne pepper
¼ teaspoon turmeric
150 ml (5 fl oz/⅔ cup) vegetable stock
salt and pepper

Trim the courgettes (zucchini) and grate them coarsely.

Seed and chop pepper (capsicum) finely. Chop onion finely and crush garlic. In a saucepan, melt low fat spread over a low heat. Add courgettes (zucchini), pepper (capsicum), onion and garlic and cook for 5 minutes, stirring.

Stir in spices, stock and salt and pepper and mix well. Bring slowly to the boil, cover and simmer for 25 minutes, stirring occasionally. Remove pan from heat and set aside to cool. Once cool, purée mixture in a blender or food processor until smooth. Return the sauce to a saucepan. Reheat gently and adjust the seasoning before serving. Serve with seafood, fish or meat.

Makes 500 ml (18 fl oz/2¼ cups/33 tbsp).

Calories per tablespoon: 8 Kcals/34 Kj
Fat per tablespoon: 0.4 g

— BROCCOLI & CHEESE SAUCE —

225 g (8 oz) broccoli
3 teaspoons cornflour
150 ml (5 fl oz/²⁄₃ cup) dry white wine
1 clove garlic
150 g (5 oz) low fat soft cheese
salt and pepper

Trim broccoli and cook in a saucepan of boiling water for 10 minutes until tender. Drain, reserving 2 tablespoons of the cooking liquid. Cool the broccoli, then purée with reserved liquid in a blender or food processor until smooth. Set the puréed broccoli aside.

In a saucepan, blend cornflour with wine. Crush garlic and add to the wine mixture. Bring slowly to the boil, stirring continuously, until the mixture thickens. Simmer gently for 3 minutes.

Remove pan from heat and stir in soft cheese, puréed broccoli and salt and pepper, mixing well. Reheat gently and adjust the seasoning before serving. Serve hot or cold with poultry, beef or fish.

Makes 550 ml (20 fl oz/2½ cups/36 tbsp).

Calories per tablespoon: 13 Kcals/55 Kj
Fat per tablespoon: 0.6 g

SALSA

2 cloves garlic
1 red chilli
2 tablespoons chopped mixed fresh herbs, such as
    parsley, thyme, rosemary and chives
400 g (14 oz) can chopped tomatoes
juice of 1 lime
salt and pepper

Crush garlic and seed and finely chop the chilli.

Place garlic, chilli, chopped herbs, tomatoes, lime juice and salt and pepper in a saucepan and mix well.

Bring slowly to the boil and simmer, uncovered, for 10 minutes, stirring occasionally. The salsa may be served hot or cold. Serve with Mexican foods such as filled tortillas.

Makes 200 ml (7 fl oz/³⁄4 cup/13 tbsp).

Calories per tablespoon: 8 Kcals/34 Kj
Fat per tablespoon: 0.07 g

MINTY APPLE SAUCE

1 small onion
450 g (1 lb) cooking apples
small bunch fresh mint
25 g (1 oz/5 teaspoons) caster sugar

Chop onion finely. Peel, core and slice apples. Put onion and apples in a saucepan with 2 tablespoons water.

Cover saucepan and heat mixture gently until the apples and onion are soft. Remove pan from heat and mash the apples and onion lightly.

Chop mint finely and add to saucepan with the sugar, mixing well. Reheat sauce gently until the sugar has dissolved. Serve hot or cold with lamb or pork.

Makes 400 ml (14 fl oz/1¾ cups/26 tbsp).

Calories per tablespoon: 11 Kcals/47 Kj
Fat per tablespoon: 0.03 g

FRESH TOMATO SAUCE

6 spring onions
1 carrot
1 stick celery
1 clove garlic
1 teaspoon olive oil
700 g (1½ lb) tomatoes
1 tablespoon chopped fresh mixed herbs, such as
    parsley, thyme, rosemary and chives
1 teaspoon ground bay leaves
1 teaspoon caster sugar
2 tablespoons tomato purée (paste) (optional)
salt and pepper

Chop spring onions, carrot and celery finely. Crush garlic.

In a saucepan, heat oil for 1 minute. Add onions, carrot, celery and garlic and cook for 5 minutes, stirring. Peel and chop tomatoes roughly and add to saucepan with remaining ingredients. Bring slowly to the boil, cover and simmer for 15 minutes, stirring occasionally. Remove pan from heat and set aside to cool. Once cool, purée the mixture in a blender or food processor until smooth. Strain the puréed sauce through a nylon sieve, discarding the pulp. Return sauce to a saucepan. Reheat gently and adjust the seasoning before serving.

Serve with Greek dishes such as stuffed vine leaves or meatballs.

Makes 500 ml (18 fl oz/2¼ cups/33 tbsp).

Calories per tablespoon: 8 Kcals/34 Kj
Fat per tablespoon: 0.2 g

Note: A simple way to peel tomatoes is to place them in boiling water for about 30 seconds, then plunge them into cold water. The skins should then peel off easily.

— GREEN PEPPERCORN SAUCE —

15 g (½ oz/3 teaspoons) low fat spread
15 g (½ oz/6 teaspoons) plain flour
150 ml (5 fl oz/⅔ cup) vegetable stock
150 ml (5 fl oz/⅔ cup) semi-skimmed milk
1 tablespoon green peppercorns
25 g (1 oz/¼ cup) finely grated smoked hard cheese
salt and pepper

In a saucepan, melt low fat spread over a low heat. Whisk in flour and cook for 1 minute, whisking.

Remove pan from heat and gradually whisk in stock and milk. Bring slowly to the boil, whisking, and continue to cook until the mixture thickens. Simmer gently for 3 minutes. Remove pan from heat. Chop or crush the peppercorns.

Stir the peppercorns and cheese into the sauce, season with salt and pepper, and reheat gently, but do not allow the sauce to boil. Serve with lamb, pork or poultry.

Makes 350 ml (12 fl oz/1½ cups/23 tbsp).

Calories per tablespoon: 12 Kcals/50 Kj
Fat per tablespoon: 0.8 g

FENNEL & OLIVE SAUCE

2 bulbs fennel
25 g (1 oz/6 teaspoons) low fat spread
25 g (1 oz/¼ cup) plain flour
300 ml (10 fl oz/1¼ cups) semi-skimmed milk
20 black olives
1 teaspoon dried dill
salt and pepper

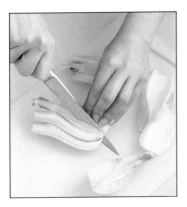

Trim and quarter fennel and cook in 300 ml (10 fl oz/1¼ cups) boiling water for 15-20 minutes until soft. Drain, reserving 150 ml (5 fl oz/⅔ cup) of the cooking liquid. Leave the cooked fennel aside to cool, then place in a blender or food processor with 3 tablespoons of the cooking liquid and purée until smooth.

In a saucepan, melt low fat spread over a low heat. Stir in flour and cook for 1 minute, stirring. Remove pan from heat and gradually stir or whisk in remaining cooking liquid and milk. Bring slowly to the boil, stirring or whisking and continue to cook until the mixture thickens. Simmer gently for 3 minutes. Stone and chop olives finely, then stir into the sauce with dill.

Stir in fennel purée and season with salt and pepper, mixing well. Reheat sauce gently and adjust the seasoning before serving. Serve with fish or poultry.

Makes 775 ml (27 fl oz/3½ cups/51 tbsp).

Calories per tablespoon: 10 Kcals/41 Kj
Fat per tablespoon: 0.5 g

—— TOMATO & BASIL SAUCE ——

6 spring onions
1 clove garlic
2 teaspoons olive oil
450 g (1 lb) tomatoes
2 tablespoons chopped fresh basil
1 tablespoon tomato purée (paste)
½ teaspoon caster sugar
12 teaspoons medium sherry
salt and pepper

Chop spring onions finely and crush garlic. In a saucepan, heat oil for 1 minute. Add onions and garlic and cook for 5 minutes, stirring.

Peel and chop tomatoes finely and add to saucepan, mixing well. Stir the basil, tomato purée (paste), sugar, sherry and salt and pepper into the tomato mixture and mix well.

Bring slowly to the boil, cover and simmer for 20 minutes, stirring occasionally. Adjust the seasoning before serving. Serve with fresh filled pasta, such as tortellini or ravioli.

Makes 600 ml (21 fl oz/2¾ cups/40 tbsp).

Calories per tablespoon: 7 Kcals/31 Kj
Fat per tablespoon: 0.3 g

Variation: Use canned tomatoes in place of fresh tomatoes.

—SMOKED HAM & LEEK SAUCE—

225 g (8 oz) leeks
25 g (1 oz/6 teaspoons) low fat spread
25 g (1 oz/¼ cup) plain flour
425 ml (15 fl oz/1¾ cups) semi-skimmed milk
175 g (6 oz) cooked smoked ham
1 tablespoon chopped fresh chives
85 g (3 oz/¾ cup) reduced-fat Cheddar cheese
salt and pepper

Chop leeks finely. In a saucepan, melt low fat spread over a low heat. Add leeks and cook for 8-10 minutes until soft, stirring.

Stir in flour and cook for 1 minute, stirring. Remove pan from heat and gradually stir in milk. Bring slowly to the boil, stirring, and continue to cook until the mixture thickens. Simmer gently for 3 minutes. Remove pan from heat.

Chop ham finely and add to the sauce with the chives. Stir in cheese and salt and pepper and mix well. Reheat the sauce gently, stirring, but do not allow the sauce to boil. Serve with vegetables such as marrow, potatoes or broccoli.

Makes 850 ml (30 fl oz/3¾ cups/56 tbsp).

Calories per tablespoon: 15 Kcals/64 Kj
Fat per tablespoon: 0.7 g

Note: This makes a very thick sauce: add extra liquid if a thinner sauce is preferred.

—— BOLOGNESE PASTA SAUCE ——

1 onion
1 clove garlic
3 teaspoons sunflower oil
2 carrots
2 sticks celery
225 g (8 oz) mushrooms
55 g (2 oz) lean back bacon
450 g (1 lb) extra lean minced beef
400 g (14 oz) can chopped tomatoes
1 tablespoon tomato purée (paste)
150 ml (5 fl oz/²⁄₃ cup) beef stock
150 ml (5 fl oz/²⁄₃ cup) dry white wine
1 teaspoon dried mixed herbs
¼ teaspoon ground bay leaves or fresh bay leaves
salt and pepper

Chop onion and crush garlic. In a large saucepan, heat oil for 1 minute. Add onion and
garlic and cook for 3 minutes, stirring. Chop
carrots and celery finely and slice mushrooms. Add to saucepan and cook for 5
minutes, stirring. Trim rind and fat from the
bacon and chop bacon finely. Add bacon to
saucepan with minced beef, mixing well.
Cook until the meat is browned all over,
stirring.

Stir in tomatoes, tomato purée (paste),
stock, wine, herbs and salt and pepper and
mix well. Bring slowly to the boil, cover and
simmer for 1½-2 hours. Remove the cover
for the last 30 minutes of the cooking time
and increase the heat slightly, to thicken the
sauce. Adjust the seasoning before serving.
Serve with freshly cooked spaghetti or pasta
shapes.

Serves 6.

Calories per serving: 207 Kcals/866 Kj
Fat per serving: 9.5 g

SMOKED FISH SAUCE

350 g (12 oz) skinned smoked haddock fillets
300 ml (10 fl oz/1¼ cups) semi-skimmed milk
1 shallot
25 g (1 oz/6 teaspoons) low fat spread
25 g (1 oz/¼ cup) plain flour
115 g (4 oz) low fat soft cheese
1 tablespoon chopped fresh tarragon
salt and pepper

Place fish in a saucepan with the milk. Bring the milk slowly to the boil, cover and simmer for 15 minutes until fish is cooked.

Strain fish, reserving milk. Flake fish. Chop shallot finely. In a saucepan, melt low fat spread over a low heat. Add shallot and cook for 5 minutes, stirring. Stir or whisk in flour and cook for 1 minute, stirring. Remove pan from heat and gradually stir or whisk in reserved milk. Bring slowly to the boil, stirring or whisking, and continue to cook until the mixture thickens. Simmer gently for 3 minutes. Remove pan from heat and stir in the fish and soft cheese, mixing well.

Stir the tarragon into the sauce and season with salt and pepper. Reheat the sauce gently and adjust the seasoning before serving. Serve with vegetable dishes or eggs and slices of toast.

Makes 700 ml (24½ fl oz/3¼ cups/46 tbsp).

Calories per tablespoon: 19 Kcals/81 Kj
Fat per tablespoon: 0.8 g

Variation: Use other types of smoked fish, such as smoked mackerel, in place of the smoked haddock.

SALMON & COURGETTE SAUCE

1 small onion
1 small courgette (zucchini)
25 g (1 oz/6 teaspoons) low fat spread
25 g (1 oz/¼ cup) plain flour
300 ml (10 fl oz/1¼ cups) semi-skimmed milk
150 ml (5 fl oz/⅔ cup) fish stock
225 g (8 oz) can red salmon
1 teaspoon dried tarragon
¼ teaspoon ground nutmeg
few drops Tabasco sauce
salt and pepper

Chop onion and courgette (zucchini) finely. In a saucepan, melt low fat spread over a low heat.

Add onion and courgette (zucchini) and cook for 8-10 minutes until soft, stirring. Stir in flour and cook for 1 minute, stirring. Remove pan from heat and gradually stir in milk and stock. Bring slowly to the boil, stirring, and continue to cook until the mixture thickens. Simmer gently for 3 minutes.

Drain, bone and flake the salmon and stir into the sauce with tarragon, nutmeg, Tabasco and salt and pepper, mixing well. Reheat the sauce gently and adjust the seasoning before serving. Serve with pasta, rice or jacket potatoes.

Makes 700 ml (24½ fl oz/3¼ cups/46 tbsp).

Calories per tablespoon: 16 Kcals/67 Kj
Fat per tablespoon: 0.8 g

OYSTER SAUCE

25 g (1 oz/6 teaspoons) low fat spread
25 g (1 oz/¼ cup) plain flour
300 ml (10 fl oz/1¼ cups) fish stock
10 fresh oysters, cooked
1 tablespoon chopped fresh parsley
finely grated rind of ½ lemon
salt and pepper

In a saucepan, melt low fat spread over a low heat. Stir in flour and cook for 1 minute, stirring. Remove pan from heat and gradually whisk in fish stock. Bring slowly to the boil, whisking, and continue to cook until the mixture thickens.

Simmer gently for 3 minutes, then remove pan from heat. Open the oysters, remove from shells and chop roughly.

Stir oysters, parsley, lemon rind and salt and pepper into the sauce and reheat gently. Adjust the seasoning before serving. Serve with fish, pasta or rice.

Makes 300 ml (10 fl oz/1¼ cups/20 tbsp).

Calories per tablespoon: 15 Kcals/64 Kj
Fat per tablespoon: 0.6 g

Note: Canned oysters can be used in place of fresh oysters, if wished.

ANCHOVY SAUCE

55 g (2 oz) can anchovies
15 g (½ oz/3 teaspoons) low fat spread
15 g (½ oz/6 teaspoons) plain flour
300 ml (10 fl oz/1¼ cups) semi-skimmed milk
1 tablespoon lemon juice
salt and pepper

Chop anchovies finely and set aside. In a
saucepan, melt low fat spread over a low heat.
Stir in flour and cook for 1 minute, stirring.
Remove pan from heat and gradually stir or
whisk in milk.

Bring slowly to the boil, stirring or whisking, and continue to cook until the mixture
thickens. Simmer gently for 3 minutes.

Add anchovies to the sauce with lemon juice
and salt and pepper, mixing well. Reheat the
sauce gently and adjust the seasoning before
serving. Serve with fish or shellfish.

Makes 350 ml (12 fl oz/1½ cups/23 tbsp).

Calories per tablespoon: 23 Kcals/95 Kj
Fat per tablespoon: 1.6 g

PLUM SAUCE

350 g (12 oz) red dessert plums
finely grated rind and juice of 1 orange
55 g (2 oz/¼ cup) caster sugar
½ teaspoon ground cinnamon
3 teaspoons brandy

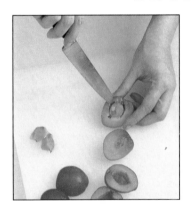

Halve and stone plums. Place plums in a saucepan with 150 ml (5 fl oz/⅔ cup) cold water.

Bring slowly to the boil, cover and simmer until the plums are soft. Remove pan from heat and set aside to cool. Once cool, purée the plums and juice in a blender or food processor until smooth.

Return the sauce to a saucepan and stir in orange rind, orange juice, sugar, cinnamon and brandy, mixing well. Reheat the sauce gently before serving. Serve with lamb, pork or beef.

Makes 550 ml (20 fl oz/2½ cups/36 tbsp).

Calories per tablespoon: 10 Kcals/41 Kj
Fat per tablespoon: 0.01 g

Note: The sauce may be served cold, if preferred.

CRANBERRY SAUCE

225 g (8 oz) cranberries
115 g (4 oz/½ cup) caster sugar
12 teaspoons ruby port

Place cranberries in a saucepan with 150 ml
(5 fl oz/⅔ cup) cold water.

Bring to the boil and boil rapidly until cranberries are soft. Reduce the heat and stir in
the sugar.

Heat gently until sugar has dissolved, then
stir in port. Reheat gently and serve with
turkey or pork.

Makes 450 ml (16 fl oz/2 cups/30 tbsp).

Calories per tablespoon: 19 Kcals/81 Kj
Fat per tablespoon: 0 g

Variation: In place of the ruby port, add
medium sherry to the sauce.

Calories per tablespoon: 19 Kcals/81 Kj
Fat per tablespoon: 0 g

SPICED APPLE SAUCE

450 g (1 lb) cooking apples
1 small onion
25 g (1 oz/6 teaspoons) low fat spread
25 g (1 oz/2 tablespoons) soft brown sugar
1 teaspoon mixed spice

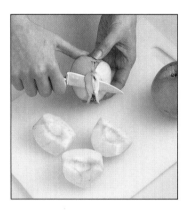

Peel, core and slice apples thinly. Chop onion finely. Place apples in a saucepan with 2 tablespoons water. Cover saucepan and cook apples gently until they are soft.

Remove pan from heat and mash thoroughly with a fork or potato masher. In a separate saucepan, melt low fat spread over a low heat. Add onion and cook gently for 8-10 minutes until soft, stirring.

Stir in puréed apples, sugar and mixed spice, mixing well. Cook gently until sugar has dissolved. Serve hot or cold with pork, gammon or goose.

Makes 600 ml (21 fl oz/2¾ cups/40 tbsp).

Calories per tablespoon: 8 Kcals/34 Kj
Fat per tablespoon: 0.3 g

BARBECUE SAUCE

2 garlic cloves
225 g (8 oz) can pineapple in fruit juice
225 g (8 oz) can chopped tomatoes
3 tablespoons cider vinegar
6 teaspoons soft brown sugar
6 teaspoons mango chutney
2 teaspoons Worcestershire sauce
½ teaspoon smooth mustard
½ teaspoon mixed spice
few drops Tabasco sauce
salt and pepper
3 teaspoons cornflour

Peel and crush garlic cloves and chop pineapple roughly.

Put garlic and pineapple in a saucepan with the tomatoes, vinegar, sugar, chutney, Worcestershire sauce, mustard, mixed spice, Tabasco sauce and salt and pepper and mix well. Bring slowly to the boil, cover and simmer gently for 10 minutes, stirring occasionally. Remove pan from heat and set aside to cool. Once cool, purée the sauce in a blender or food processor until smooth. Return the sauce to a saucepan.

In a small bowl, blend cornflour with 1 tablespoon water. Stir cornflour mixture into sauce and bring slowly to the boil, stirring continuously. Simmer gently for 3 minutes and adjust the seasoning before serving. Serve with barbecued or grilled meats such as steaks, chops or chicken portions.

Makes 400 ml (14 fl oz/1¾ cups/26 tbsp).

Calories per tablespoon: 14 Kcals/59 Kj
Fat per tablespoon: 0.1 g

GOOSEBERRY SAUCE

450 g (1 lb) gooseberries
finely grated rind and juice of 1 orange
25 g (1 oz/6 teaspoons) low fat spread
25 g (1 oz/2 tablespoons) soft brown sugar
¼ teaspoon ground nutmeg

Place gooseberries in a saucepan with orange rind and juice and 150 ml (5 fl oz/²⁄₃ cup) water, mixing well. Bring the mixture slowly to the boil, cover saucepan and simmer gently for 5-10 minutes until the gooseberries are cooked, stirring occasionally.

Remove the pan from the heat and set aside to cool. Once cool, purée the gooseberries in a blender or food processor until smooth. Return the mixture to a saucepan.

Stir in low fat spread, sugar and nutmeg. Bring slowly to the boil, stirring, and simmer gently for 1 minute. Serve with oily fish such as mackerel.

Makes 500 ml (18 fl oz/2¼ cups/33 tbsp).

Calories per tablespoon: 9 Kcals/36 Kj
Fat per tablespoon: 0.4 g

CUMBERLAND SAUCE

finely grated rind and juice of 1 orange
finely grated rind and juice of 1 lemon
12 teaspoons redcurrant jelly
2 tablespoons red wine vinegar
1 teaspoon smooth mustard
salt and pepper
3 teaspoons cornflour
12 teaspoons ruby port

Put orange rind and juice, lemon rind and juice, redcurrant jelly, red wine vinegar, mustard, salt and pepper and 4 tablespoons water in a bowl and mix well.

Pour mixture into a saucepan. Bring slowly to the boil, stirring. Cover and simmer for 5 minutes, stirring occasionally. In a small bowl, blend cornflour with 1 tablespoon water and port. Stir cornflour mixture into the sauce, mixing well.

Bring slowly to the boil, stirring continuously, until the mixture thickens. Simmer gently for 3 minutes. Remove pan from heat and adjust the seasoning before serving. Serve hot or cold with ham, pork, game or offal.

Makes 500 ml (18 fl oz/2¼ cups/33 tbsp).

Calories per tablespoon: 10 Kcals/41 Kj
Fat per tablespoon: 0.01 g

FIG SAUCE

2 shallots or 1 onion
225 g (8 oz) dried figs
2 teaspoons olive oil
300 ml (10 fl oz/1¼ cups) chicken stock
2 tablespoons cider vinegar
1 tablespoon chopped fresh thyme
salt and pepper

Chop shallots or onion finely and chop figs roughly. In a saucepan, heat oil for 1 minute. Add shallots or onion and figs and cook for 5 minutes, stirring.

Stir in stock, vinegar, thyme and salt and pepper and mix well. Bring slowly to the boil, cover and simmer for 10 minutes, stirring occasionally. Remove pan from heat and set aside to cool.

Once cool, purée the mixture in a blender or food processor until smooth. Return sauce to a saucepan. Reheat gently and adjust the seasoning before serving. Serve hot or cold with lamb or beef.

Makes 500 ml (18 fl oz/2¼ cups/33 tbsp).

Calories per tablespoon: 18 Kcals/75 Kj
Fat per tablespoon: 0.4 g

— BLACKBERRY & APPLE SAUCE —

225 g (8 oz) cooking apples
225 g (8 oz) blackberries
55 g (2 oz/¼ cup) caster sugar
115 g (4 oz) low fat soft cheese
150 ml (5 fl oz/⅔ cup) reduced fat single (light) cream

Peel, core and slice apples thinly. Put apples and blackberries in a saucepan with 3 tablespoons water. Cover and cook gently until fruit is soft, stirring occasionally.

Remove pan from heat and stir in sugar. Set aside to cool. Once cool, purée the fruit in a blender or food processor until smooth. Press the fruit through a nylon sieve, discarding pips.

Whisk soft cheese and cream together, then whisk fruit in, mixing thoroughly. Serve with steamed and baked puddings, meringues or poached fruit such as peaches or pears.

Makes 550 ml (20 fl oz/2½ cups/36 tbsp).

Calories per tablespoon: 20 Kcals/83 Kj
Fat per tablespoon: 0.9 g

Variation: In place of blackberries, use raspberries, loganberries or blackcurrants.

GINGER SAUCE

55 g (2 oz/¼ cup) caster sugar
55 g (2 oz) preserved stem ginger
12 teaspoons syrup from stem ginger
2 tablespoons lemon juice
1 teaspoon arrowroot

Put sugar in a saucepan with 150 ml (5 fl oz/ ⅔ cup) water. Heat gently until sugar has dissolved, stirring, then bring to the boil and boil for 5 minutes.

Chop stem ginger finely and stir into sugar mixture with ginger syrup and lemon juice, mixing well. In a small bowl, blend arrowroot with 1 tablespoon water until smooth.

Stir arrowroot mixture into the sauce. Reheat gently, stirring continuously, until sauce thickens. Serve with fresh melon, fresh fruit salad or hot steamed puddings.

Makes 225 ml (8 fl oz/¾ cup/15 tbsp).

Calories per tablespoon: 29 Kcals/121 Kj
Fat per tablespoon: 0.02 g

MANGO SAUCE

1 mango
45 g (1½ oz/3 tablespoons) low fat spread
55 g (2 oz/½ cup) plain flour
450 ml (16 fl oz/2 cups) semi-skimmed milk
55 g (2 oz/⅓ cup) soft brown sugar

Peel and stone mango and chop flesh roughly. Place mango in a blender or food processor and blend until smooth. Set aside. In a saucepan, melt low fat spread over a low heat. Stir in flour and cook for 1 minute, stirring.

Remove pan from heat and gradually whisk in the milk. Bring slowly to the boil, whisking, and continue to cook until mixture thickens. Simmer gently for 3 minutes.

Remove pan from heat and stir in puréed mango and sugar, mixing well. Reheat the sauce gently before serving. Serve with tropical fresh fruit salad or fruit compote.

Makes 700 ml (24½ fl oz/3¼ cups/46 tbsp).

Calories per tablespoon: 20 Kcals/83 Kj
Fat per tablespoon: 0.6 g

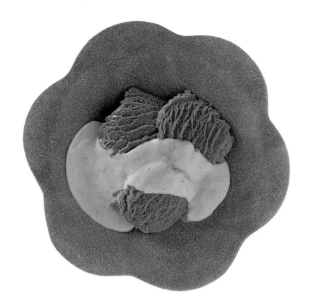

—BANANA & GINGER SAUCE—

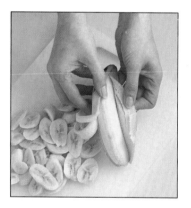

3 bananas, approximately 450 g (1 lb) in weight
juice of 1 lemon
juice of 1 lime
450 ml (16 fl oz/2 cups) low fat plain yogurt
12 teaspoons soft brown sugar
2 teaspoons ground ginger

Peel and slice bananas. Put bananas, lemon juice and lime juice in a blender or food processor and blend until smooth.

Add yogurt, sugar and ginger to the blender or food processor and blend mixture until thoroughly mixed.

Pour sauce into a suitable serving dish, cover and leave the sauce in a cool place for 30 minutes before serving, to allow the flavours to develop. Serve with fresh fruit, low fat ice cream or frozen yogurt.

Makes 700 ml (24½ fl oz/3¼ cups/46 tbsp).

Calories per tablespoon: 17 Kcals/70 Kj
Fat per tablespoon: 0.1 g

- STRAWBERRY & LEMON SAUCE -

225 g (8 oz) strawberries
finely grated rind and juice of 2 lemons
55 g (2 oz/¼ cup) caster sugar
1 teaspoon arrowroot

Put strawberries in a blender or food processor and blend until smooth. Set aside. Pour into a saucepan.

Add 150 ml (5 fl oz/⅔ cup) water to the saucepan and stir in lemon rind, lemon juice and sugar. Heat gently, stirring, until sugar has dissolved, then bring mixture to the boil and simmer gently for 5 minutes. In a small bowl, blend arrowroot with 1 tablespoon water until smooth.

Stir arrowroot mixture into the saucepan, mixing well. Reheat the sauce gently until mixture thickens, stirring continuously. Serve with fruit jelly, fresh fruit, fruit tart or sorbet.

Makes 450 ml (16 fl oz/2 cups/30 tbsp).

Calories per tablespoon: 10 Kcals/41 Kj
Fat per tablespoon: 0.008 g

VANILLA YOGURT SAUCE

150 ml (5 fl oz/²⁄₃ cup) semi-skimmed milk
1 vanilla pod
1 teaspoon cornflour
55 g (2 oz/¹⁄₃ cup) icing sugar
300 ml (10 fl oz/1 ¼ cups) low fat plain yogurt

In a saucepan, warm milk. Split vanilla pod lengthways and add to milk. Remove pan from heat, cover and set aside to infuse for 15 minutes.

Remove vanilla pod and scrape seeds from pod into milk. In a small bowl, blend cornflour with 1 tablespoon water until smooth. Stir cornflour mixture into milk and bring slowly to the boil, stirring continuously, until mixture thickens. Simmer sauce gently for 3 minutes, stirring.

Remove pan from heat, pour sauce into a bowl and set aside to cool. Sift icing sugar into a bowl. Once the cornflour sauce is cool, stir in the icing sugar and yogurt and mix thoroughly. Serve with hot or cold puddings or meringues.

Makes 430 ml (15 fl oz/1¾ cups/28 tbsp).

Calories per tablespoon: 17 Kcals/70 Kj
Fat per tablespoon: 0.2 g

BLACKCURRANT SAUCE

225 g (8 oz) blackcurrants
9 teaspoons clear honey
6 teaspoons blackcurrant liqueur, such as Cassis
1 teaspoon arrowroot

Top and tail blackcurrants and place in a saucepan with honey and 4 tablespoons water. Cover and cook mixture gently until blackcurrants are soft, stirring occasionally.

Remove pan from heat and stir in blackcurrant liqueur. In a small bowl, blend arrowroot with 1 tablespoon water until smooth. Stir arrowroot mixture into blackcurrants and mix well.

Bring slowly to the boil, stirring continuously, until sauce thickens. Serve hot or cold with frozen yogurt or fresh fruit such as figs.

Makes 450 ml (16 fl oz/2 cups/30 tbsp).

Calories per tablespoon: 9 Kcals/36 Kj
Fat per tablespoon: 0 g

INDEX